Elkton, MD 21921

Life Under the Sea

Octopuses

by Cari Meister

Bullfrog Books

Ideas for Parents and Teachers

Bullfrog Books give children practice reading informational text at the earliest levels. Repetition, familiar words, and photo labels support early readers.

Before Reading

- Discuss the cover photo. What does it tell them?
- Look at the picture glossary together. Read and discuss the words.

Read the Book

- "Walk" through the book and look at the photos. Let the child ask questions.
- Read the book to the child, or have him or her read independently.

After Reading

- Prompt the child to think more. Ask: What do you find most amazing about the octopus? Why?

Bullfrog Books are published by Jump!
5357 Penn Avenue South
Minneapolis, MN 55419
www.jumplibrary.com

Library of Congress Cataloging-in-Publication Data
Meister, Cari.
 Octopuses / by Cari Meister.
   p. cm. -- (Bullfrog books: life under the sea)
 Summary: "This photo-illustrated nonfiction story for young readers describes octopuses' behavior and how they defend themselves from predators. Includes picture glossary"--Provided by publisher.
 Includes bibliographical references and index.
 ISBN 978-1-62031-010-6 (hbk. : alk. paper)
 1. Octopuses--Juvenile literature. I. Title.
 QL430.3.O2M45 2013
 594'.56--dc23
                                    2012008428

Series Editor: Rebecca Glaser
Series Designer: Ellen Huber
Production: Chelsey Luther

Photo Credits: Dreamstime.com, 7, 14-15, 16-17, 19; Getty Images, 1, 8, 18, 21, 22, 23tl; iStockphoto, 24; National Geographic Stock, cover; Shutterstock, 3r, 3l, 4, 5, 10, 11, 12-13, 20, 21, 22 inset, 23bl, 23br, 23tr; SuperStock, 6-7, 8-9

Printed in the United States of America at Corporate Graphics in North Mankato, Minnesota
7-2012/ PO 1125
10 9 8 7 6 5 4 3 2 1

Table of Contents

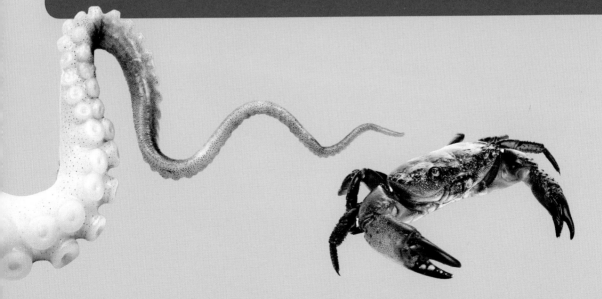

Octopuses Under the Sea

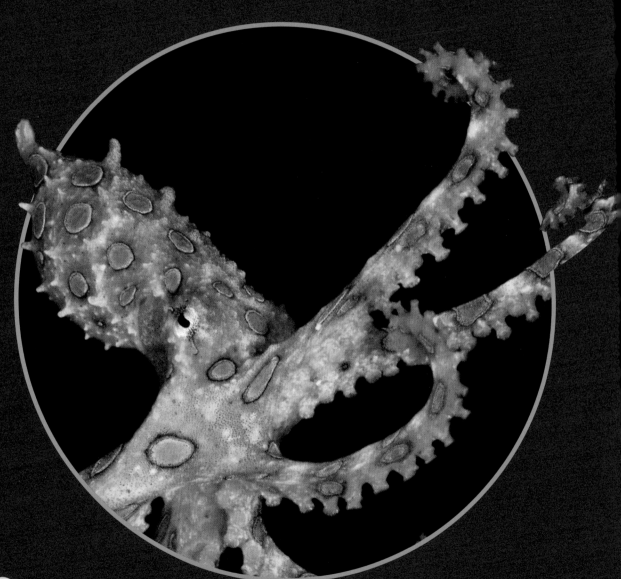

An octopus hunts.
His eyes look.
His eight arms
feel the sand.

5

A crab!
It tries to get away.

The octopus has
suction cups.

They hold on.

suction
cup

Now he uses his beak.
It breaks the shell.

beak

He drops the crab.
He turns white.
He is scared!

He squirts ink.
It puzzles the shark.

12

But the fight
is not over.

The shark bites
off his arm.

It's okay.

He can grow
a new arm.

He just needs
to hide and rest.

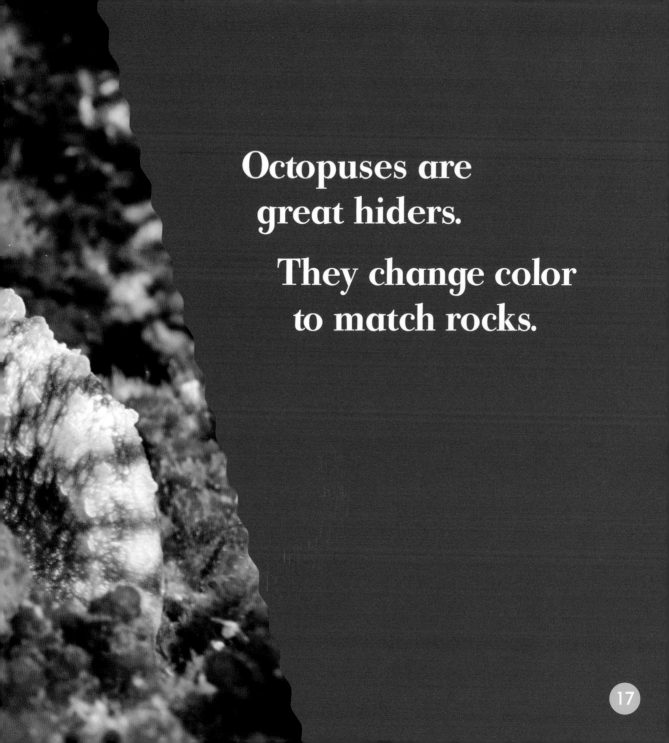

Octopuses are
great hiders.

They change color
to match rocks.

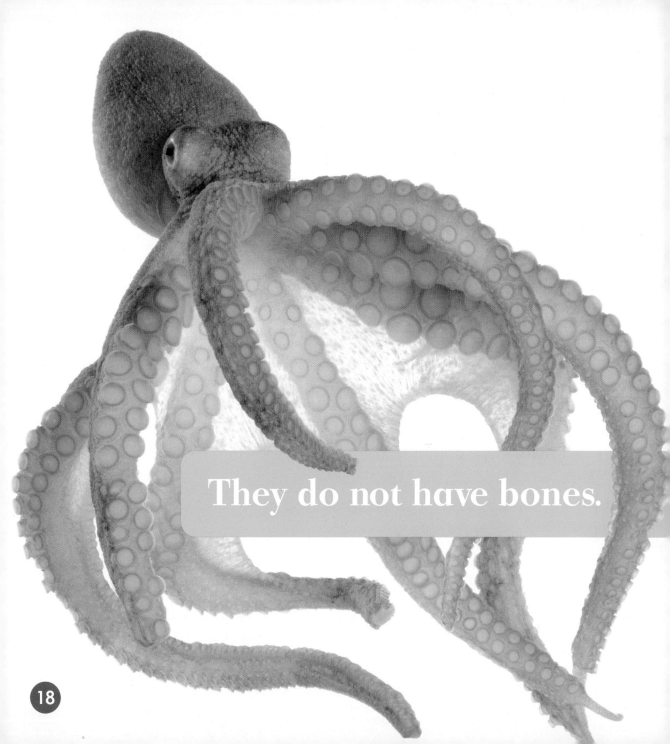

They do not have bones.

They squeeze into small spaces.

Here's a cave!

Now he's safe.

Parts of an Octopus

arms
The eight long body parts that help an octopus move.

eye
A body part used to see.

suction cups
The strong suckers on the bottom of an octopus' arms.

22

Picture Glossary

beak
The hard part of an octopus' mouth on the underside of its body.

cave
A hole in the side of a cliff. It may be under water.

bone
A hard body part that makes up a skeleton; octopuses have no bones.

ink
The dark liquid that an octopus squirts out when in danger.

Index

To Learn More

Learning more is as easy as 1, 2, 3.

1) Go to www.factsurfer.com

2) Enter "octopus" into the search box.

3) Click the "Surf" button to see a list of websites.

With factsurfer.com, finding more information is just a click away.